ROBOTS
SENSING AND DOING

WORLD BOOK

www.worldbook.com

Co-published by agreement between Shi Tu Hui and World Book, Inc.

Shi Tu Hui
Room 1807, Block 1,
#3 West Dawang Road
Chaoyang District, Beijing 100025
P.R. China

World Book, Inc.
180 North LaSalle Street
Suite 900
Chicago, Illinois 60601
USA

© 2026. All rights reserved. This volume may not be reproduced in whole or in part in any form without prior written permission from the publisher.

WORLD BOOK and the GLOBE DEVICE are registered trademarks or trademarks of World Book, Inc.

Library of Congress Control Number: 2025938164

Robots
ISBN: 978-0-7166-5814-6 (set, hard cover)

Robots Sensing and Doing
ISBN: 978-0-7166-5816-0 (hard cover)

Also available as:
ISBN: 978-0-7166-5826-9 (soft cover)
ISBN: 978-0-7166-5836-8 (e-book)

WORLD BOOK STAFF

Writer: Jeff De La Rosa

Editorial

Vice President
Tom Evans

Senior Manager, New Content
Jeff De La Rosa

Associate Manager, New Content
William D. Adams

Content Creator
Elizabeth Huyck

Proofreader
Nathalie Strassheim

Graphics and Design

*Senior Visual
Communications Designer*
Melanie Bender

Photo Editor
Rosalia Bledsoe

ACKNOWLEDGMENTS

Cover: © 35lab/Shutterstock; © SoftBank Robotics; © Wellphoto/Alamy Images; © The Shadow Robot Company

4-5 © Mike Dotta, Shutterstock
6-7 © Igor Podgorny, Shutterstock; © Lecter/Shutterstock
8-9 Andreas Dantz (licensed under CC BY 2.0)
10-11 © iRobot Corporation
12-13 MTheiler (licensed under CC BY-SA 4.0); © Wellphoto/Alamy Images
14-15 © Vchal/Shutterstock; © VTT Studio/Shutterstock
16-17 © Velodyne LIDAR
18-19 © MetraLabs GmbH
20-21 © Honda Research Institute Japan
22-23 © iRobot Corporation
24-25 © SoftBank Robotics; Peter Schulz (licensed under CC BY-SA 4.0)
26-27 © Ociacia/Shutterstock
28-29 © Asharkyu/Shutterstock; © Boston Dynamics
30-31 © KAIST
32-33 © Universal Pictures; © Festo
34-35 © Harvard Microrobotics Laboratory
36-37 © M. Zeta, Shutterstock
38-39 © Asharkyu/Shutterstock
40-41 © Sspopov/Shutterstock; © Goudsmit Magnetics Group
42-43 © The Shadow Robot Company
44-45 © Miso Robotics
46-47 © tdee photo cm/Shutterstock

Contents

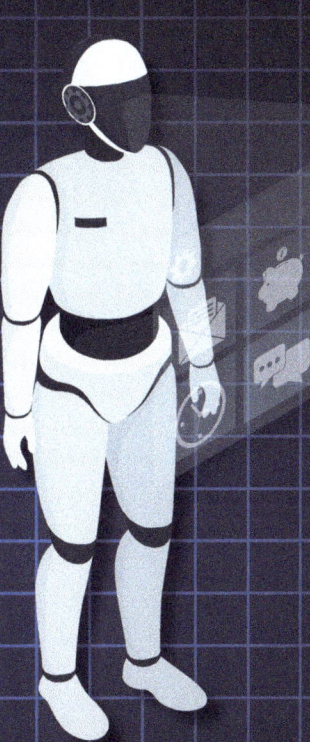

- 4 Introduction
- 6 Robot Senses
- 8 Bump and Go
- 10 Too Close for Comfort
- 12 ROBOT CHALLENGE: Seeing Things
- 14 Familiar Faces
- 16 Lidar
- 18 HELLO, MY NAME IS: Tory
- 20 I'm Listening!
- 22 Inside and Out
- 26 Actuators
- 28 Degrees of Freedom
- 30 HELLO, MY NAME IS: DRC-Hubo
- 32 Air and Liquid Power
- 34 Piezoelectrics
- 36 End Effectors
- 38 ROBOT CHALLENGE: Get a Grip!
- 40 Grippers
- 42 HELLO, MY NAME IS: The Shadow Dexterous Hand
- 44 Other End Effectors
- 46 Hands-On Robotics
- 48 Glossary and Index

Terms defined in the glossary are in type **that looks like this** on their first appearance on any spread (two facing pages).

Introduction

Every day, we interact with the world around us. We do this mostly using our senses and our muscles. Senses—such as sight, hearing, and touch—enable us to figure out what is going on in our surroundings. Muscles help us move around, pick things up, and otherwise change our environment.

Robots also interact with the world through senses and motion. A robot's "senses" are provided by devices called **sensors.** A sensor is a device that detects something, such as light, heat, motion, temperature, or vibration.

A robot's "muscles" are provided by **actuators.** An actuator is a device that moves something. The most common kind of actuator is an **electric motor.** But actuators can also be powered by air, fluids under pressure, or other sources.

Little learner
The robot iCub is designed to "learn" about the world through sensing and doing, much as a child does. Robots use sensors to detect their surroundings and actuators (robotic "muscles") to interact with them.

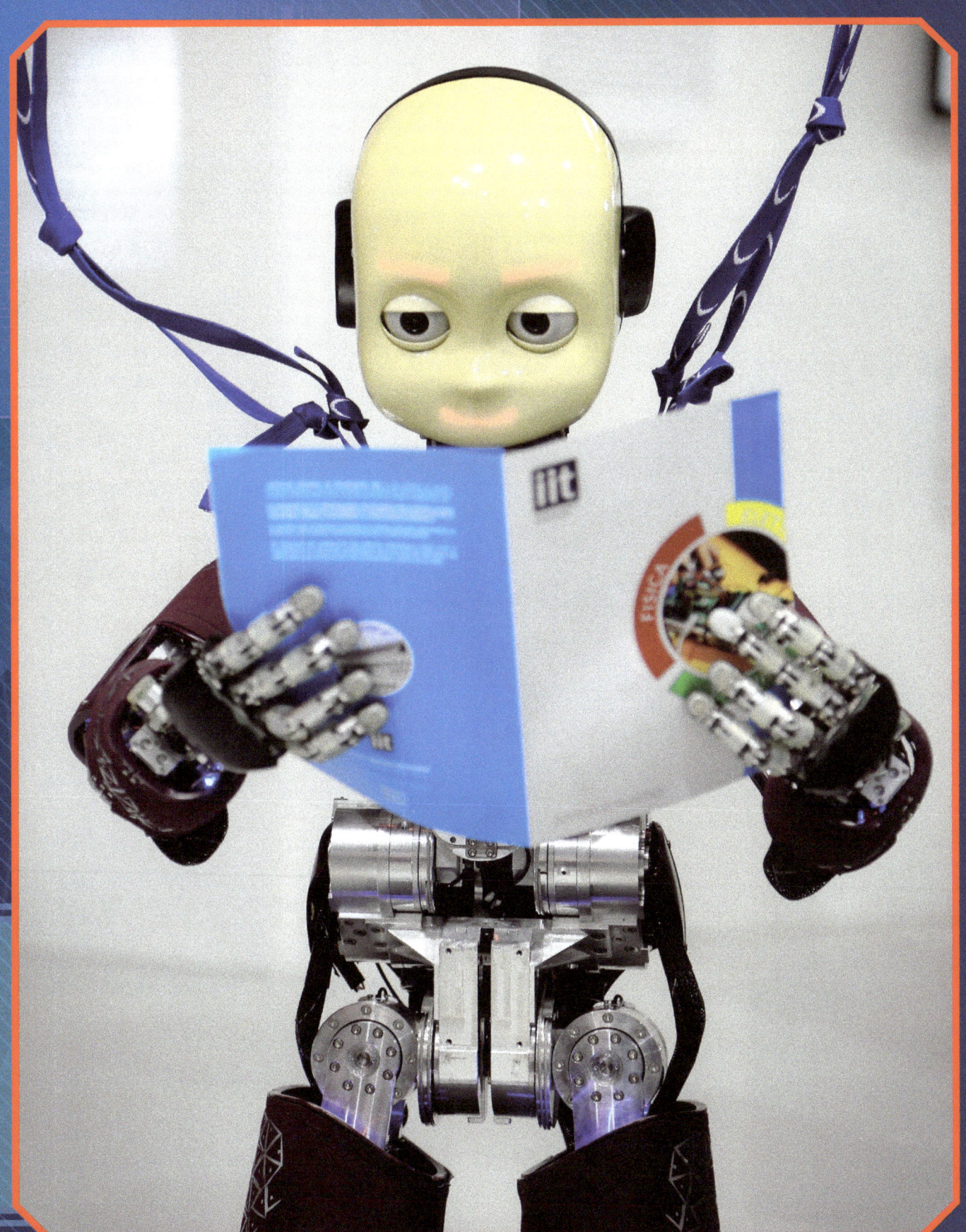

Robot Senses

Human beings generally share a common set of senses. But a robot's sensors can be chosen to fit its specific needs.

A robot's sensors might include cameras, gas sensors, microphones, electronic touch sensors, pressure sensors, and many others.

Robots often have multiple sensors spaced all over their bodies. They might have cameras in their hands or smell sensors in their feet, if that's useful for the robot.

These sensors are often very small—sometimes many live on a single computer chip. This microchip contains a gyroscope, accelerometer, compass, and barometer.

VISION

- Two cameras for 3D vision
- IR and UV cameras
- Lidar

Some robots cameras can detect wavelengths human eyes can't see.

TOUCH

- Pressure sensors
- Proximity sensors
- Heat sensors
- Electromagnetic sensors
- Vibration sensors

ENERGY LEVEL

- Battery monitor

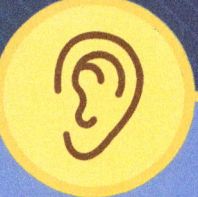

HEARING

- Microphones (several, around the body)
- Vibration sensors

TASTE, SMELL

- Gas sensors
- Liquid sensors
- Spectrometer
- Smoke detector

PROPRIOCEPTION
(how your body is moving)

- IMU (inertial measurement unit)
- Gyroscopes (measure tipping)
- Accelerometers
- Pressure sensors
- Bend sensors
- Distance counter

Bump  and Go

Sometimes engineers may try to give a robot the simplest set of **sensors** it needs to do its job well.

Think about a simple robotic floor vacuum. The first such vacuums basically wandered around the room at random. When they bumped into something, they simply took a turn and moved on. Such a robot needs only a simple bumper sensor. The sensor alerts the robot when it bumps into something. The robot can then back up and turn in another direction.

Robotic vacuums also use simple sensors to keep from driving off a ledge or tumbling down stairs. These are called **cliff sensors.** A cliff sensor shines a light on the floor. The floor reflects the light back to a detector. If the floor drops away sharply, the light is not reflected to the detector. The detector alerts the robot, which can stop to avoid falling.

Random acts of clean-ness
Glowing lines reveal the path taken by a robotic vacuum cleaner wandering pretty much at random. A simple bumper sensor alerts the robot when to turn.

Too Close for Comfort

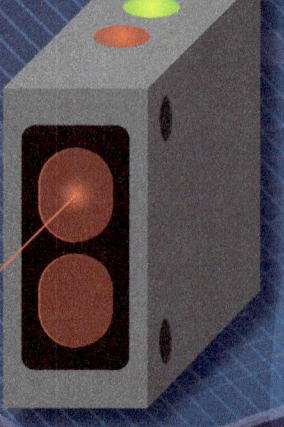

A **cliff sensor** is a simple kind of **proximity sensor.** *Proximity* means *nearness.* A proximity sensor tells a robot how near something is. A cliff sensor detects how near the floor is. Robots use other proximity sensors to detect obstacles before they run into them.

Proximity sensors work in a variety of ways. Many make use of reflected light, much like a cliff sensor. The sensor gives off light. The light bounces off the robot's surroundings. The reflected light is gathered by a detector. The closer an object is, the brighter the reflection will be. This kind of sensor is usually tuned to a very specific frequency of light. This helps to prevent light from other sources from confusing the sensor.

Other proximity sensors make use of ultrasound. Ultrasound is sound that is too high-pitched to be heard by the human ear. The sensor gives off ultrasound, which echoes off the robot's surroundings. A microphone measures the reflected echo to determine proximity.

Cliffhanger
A tumble down the stairs could spell certain doom for a robotic vacuum cleaner. A cliff sensor helps it to detect (and avoid) sharp drops.

[11]

ROBOT CHALLENGE

Seeing Things

Wouldn't it be easier if a robot could just see its surroundings, the way people do? Indeed, many robots "see" through the use of digital cameras. But seeing is not as simple as it sounds.

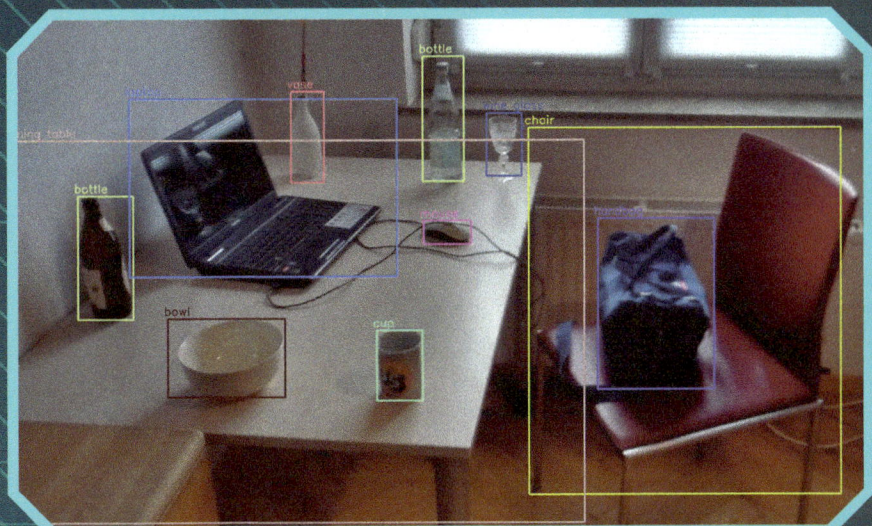

The world around us is filled with a great variety of things. These things are constantly changing in appearance due to changes in position, viewing angle, and lighting. Human brains are great at making sense of this shifting confusion of shapes. Robots find it much more difficult to sort out what they are seeing.

Robots generally simplify visual information by focusing on particular features. For example, a robot may try to find the edges of objects. This can help the robot navigate its surroundings. Advances in **artificial intelligence** are helping robots get better at identifying what they see. But this requires a lot of computing power. For many jobs, proximity sensors are good enough.

Eye spy...what?
Cameras provide robots with visual information. Powerful computer programs help them recognize what they're looking at.

Familiar Faces

Facial recognition is the ability to identify and remember faces. When human beings look at faces, we take in huge amounts of visual information. This ability makes us good at remembering faces. It also helps us to gather information—such as age, sex, and mood—from faces we have never seen.

Robots tend to see faces a little differently. Their software identifies and measures features common among faces. A robot might measure the distance between the eyes, the width of the nose, and the length of the jawline, for example. By comparing many

"I'd recognize that pupillary distance anywhere"
Robots recognize faces by measuring the distance between features, such as the distance between the eyes (called pupillary distance).

such measures, robots are able to match individuals to face pictures in its database. Some robots are even able to read facial expressions to judge a person's mood. This allows robots to greet people by name and interact in a more humanlike way.

Robots use similar techniques for recognizing other objects in the environment. They try to match the mathematical profile of an image to a large database of possible things.

"Nice to see you again!" The small robot Pepper can remember faces and respond to each individual differently. Some companies use Pepper to greet people and help customers.

Lidar

Another method robots use to see what's around them is **lidar** (pronounced *LY dahr*). *Lidar* stands for *light detection* and *ranging*.

A lidar system gives off short pulses of infrared laser light. These pulses reflect off the robot's surroundings. The reflections are detected by a light **sensor.** By measuring how long it takes for light to bounce back from an object, the lidar unit can determine how far away an object is.

A lidar unit can include dozens of light sensors. Some spin to sweep an area many times a second. This gives the robot a detailed picture of its surroundings as it moves around. Lidar also works in the dark, unlike visual sensors. But it can be confused by rain.

Lidar-vision
This image was made by a spinning lidar system in the center of the black circle. Measuring laser reflections reveals cars, trees, and other objects.

HELLO, MY NAME IS:

Tory

Robots can see in many different ways. Some stores use a robot named Tory to count their inventory, the unsold goods sitting on racks and shelves. After the store closes, Tory rolls up and down the aisles, counting clothes, shoes, toys, or other goods. Tory conducts its counts using a technology called RFID. *RFID* stands for *r*adio *f*requency *id*entification. Special RFID tags on the unsold items give off a radio signal as Tory approaches. Tory uses these signals to identify and count the goods. Other inventory robots take photos of shelves and use object recognition AI to determine what's there.

AUTONOMY
HIGH
Tory conducts its counts without the need for human assistance.

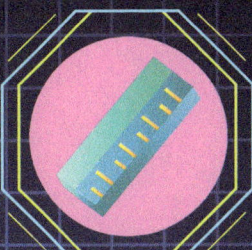
SIZE
5 feet (1.5 meters) tall

PERSONALITY TYPE
Night owl. Tory stays up working while shoppers are fast asleep.

MAKER
The German company MetraLabs manufactures Tory.

SPEED COUNTER
Tory can count inventory 10 times faster than human workers.

WHAT'S IN A NAME?
Tory's name comes from Inven*tory*.

[19]

I'm Listening!

Another important robot sense is hearing. Microphones are **sensors** that pick up sound waves and convert them into electrical signals. A computer can analyze these signals for patterns created by specific sounds.

Many robots use microphones for **voice recognition.** They analyze sounds for patterns that match particular words. Voice recognition enables robots to respond to spoken commands. Being able to hear sirens, people, weather, and other vehicles is also important for robot cars.

Listening is more complicated than just hearing. Humans are good at telling the difference between important sounds and background noise. But this can be challenging for a robot.

In 2012, the Honda Research Institute in Wako, Japan, used a robot called HEARBO to try to improve robot hearing. HEARBO used multiple microphones to pinpoint the source of particular sounds. This helped HEARBO to focus on the sound and filter out background noise. Work on robot hearing is also helping to make better hearing aids.

I'm hearing things
The robot HEARBO is bristling with microphones. It can use them to zero in on the source of a particular sound and to filter out background noise.

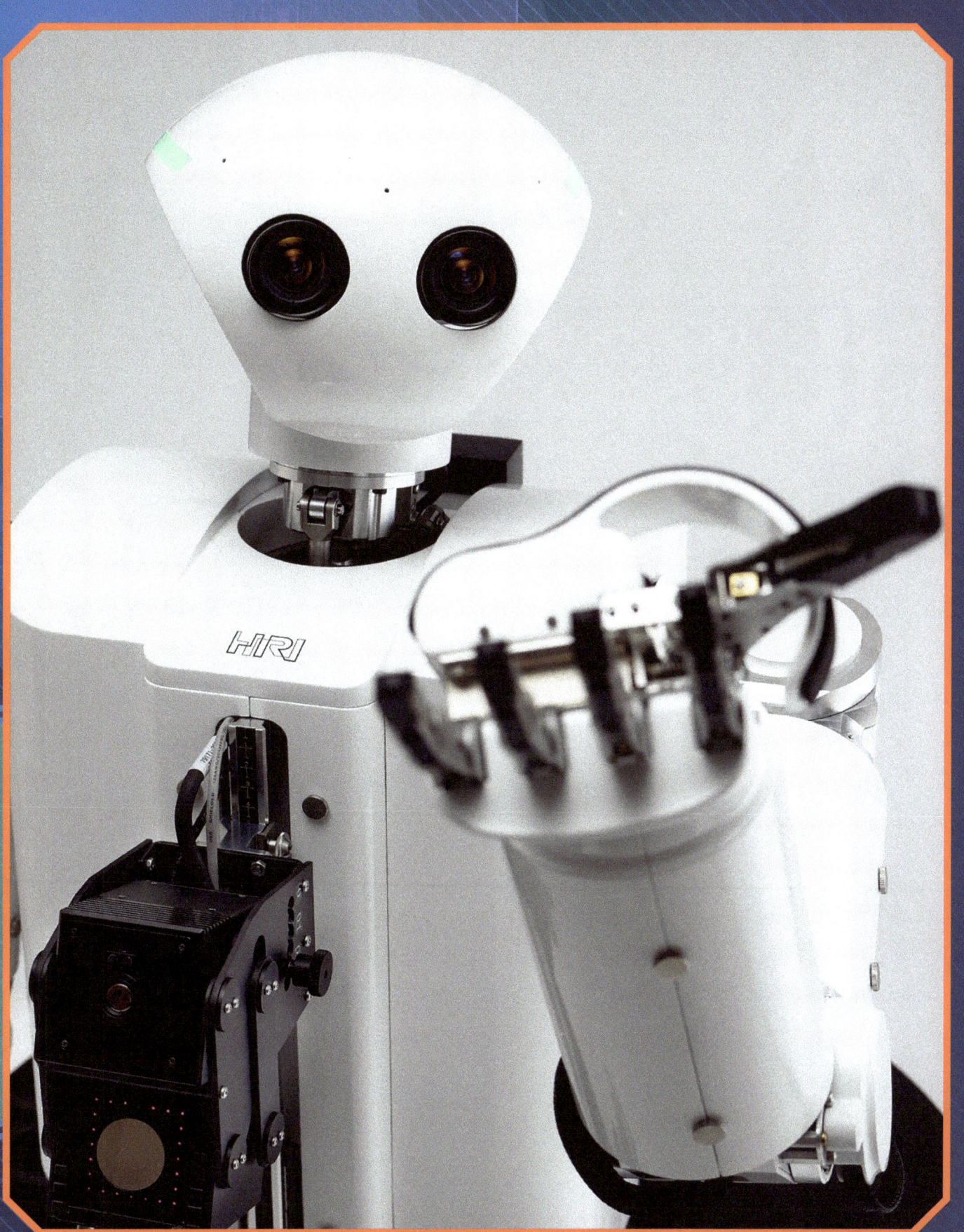

Inside and Out

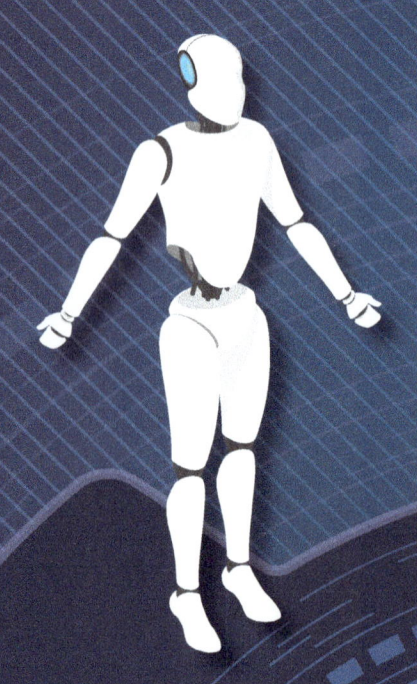

When you think about senses, you probably think of sight, hearing, touch, taste, and smell. These *external* (outside) senses mainly tell you about the world around you. But you also have *internal* (inside) senses that tell you about the condition of your body. You have a sense of balance, for example. You also have a sense of what your arms, legs, and other body parts are doing.

Cameras, microphones, and **lidar** are some of a robot's external **sensors.** But a robot may also have internal sensors that monitor conditions inside.

Some internal sensors measure the positions of a robot's various joints. These sensors help the robot keep track of its own body position. Other sensors may measure **torque** at a particular joint. Such sensors measure how much force a robot is using. They can tell a robot how much weight it is lifting or how hard it is pushing on something.

Time to recharge
Imagine a robotic vacuum cleaner that wandered around until it ran out of energy. You would keep having to find it and plug it in. Instead, a robotic vacuum keeps track of its battery power. When it senses that that the juice is running low, it makes its way back to the charging port.

Human-shaped robots use many internal **sensors** to track the position and **torque** at joints. Being able to precisely sense motion, contact, and how hard they are gripping helps these robots avoid injuring human coworkers.

Robots that move around a lot may rely on such internal sensors as **accelerometers** and **gyrometers.**

Accelerometers detect *acceleration.* Acceleration is a change in motion, whether speeding up, slowing down, or changing direction. The downward pull of gravity is a form of acceleration, so an accelerometer can also detect which way is down. This can help a robot avoid tipping.

A gyrometer measures rotation. It can help a robot sense when it is spinning or tipping.

The pint-sized robot Nao is a **humanoid** robot that walks on two legs. This requires great balance to keep from toppling over. Nao relies on both an accelerometer and a gyrometer to keep the robot on its feet.

The robot Nao has many internal sensors that help it to remain upright, even when playing soccer (opposite). But if all else fails, Nao has an important skill: the ability to stand itself back up (below).

Actuators

A robot's senses help tell it what to do, but to get the job done a robot needs to move, move, move. We human beings move through the use of our muscles. A robot's "muscles" are called **actuators.** An actuator is any part of the robot that powers movement.

Most actuators are small **electric motors.** An electric motor uses electric energy to produce rotation, or spinning motion. A simple actuator of this type might serve as the "elbow" on a robotic arm. Spinning in one direction causes the elbow to bend. Spinning the other causes the arm to straighten out.

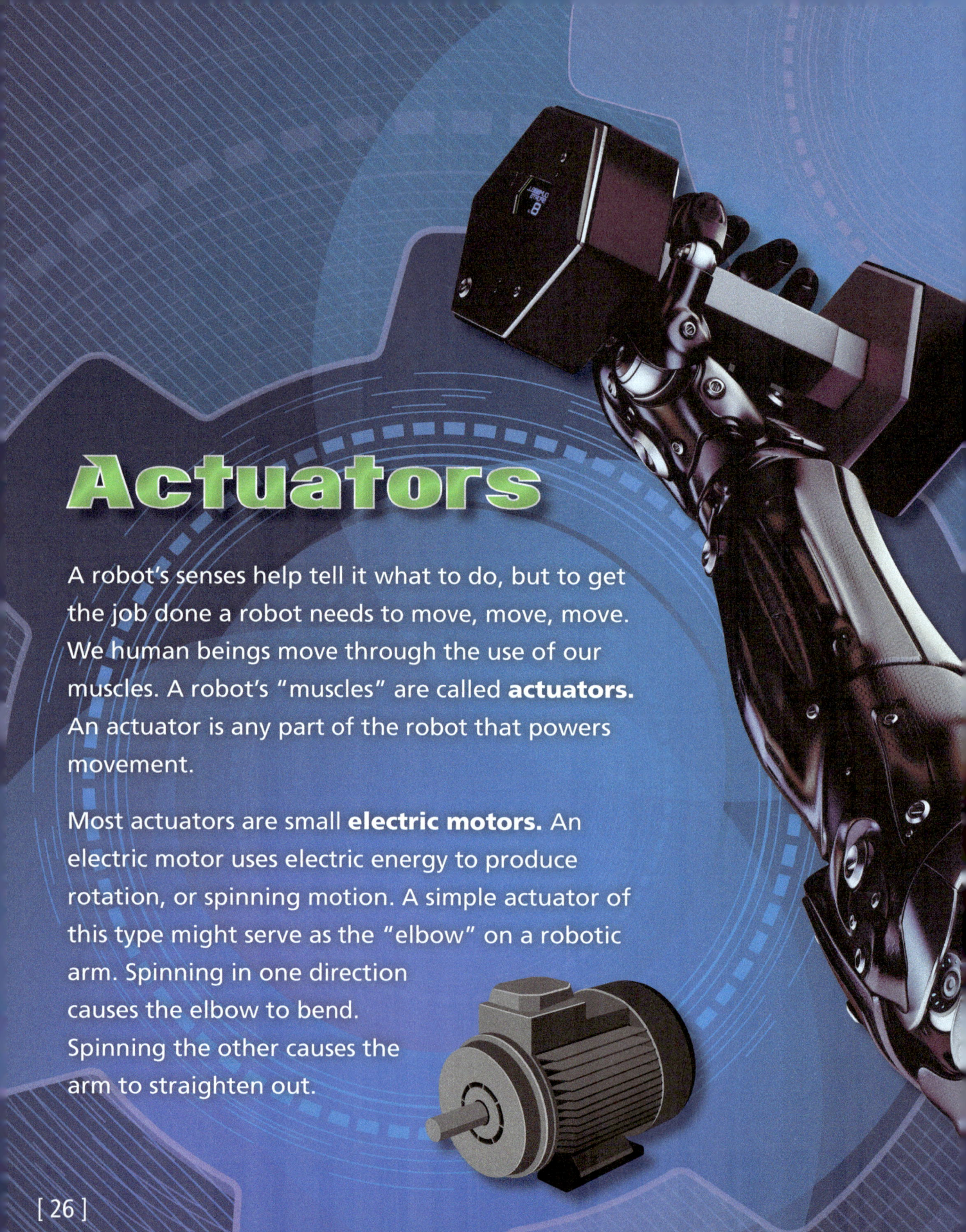

Degrees of Freedom

Imagine a robotic arm whose only **actuator** was a single **electric motor**. The arm could only bend and unbend in one direction, kind of like a human elbow. But the elbow is not the only joint in the human body. Likewise, robots are often designed with multiple joints and actuators. Each additional actuator allows a robotic joint to rotate in another direction.

Elbow 'bot
A robot with a single joint is not very flexible. Most robots, such as this industrial robot, have at least a few degrees of freedom.

Freedom to move
The walking humanoid robot Atlas has joints in roughly the same places humans do. But Atlas's joints can turn all the way around, allowing it to do acrobatics impossible for a human.

The ability to rotate in a single direction is called a **degree of freedom.** So a robot arm with five rotating actuators is said to have five degrees of freedom.

The more degrees of freedom a robot has, the more complex the movements it can make. A simple robotic arm might have only two or three degrees of freedom. A **humanoid** robot might have dozens of degrees of freedom, including several in its arms, legs, body, and face.

HELLO, MY NAME IS:

DRC-Hubo

If you want a rescue robot that can handle many different tasks, it helps to give it a flexible body. That was the winning strategy of DRC-Hubo, which took the top prize at the DARPA rescue robot challenge in 2015. DRC-Hubo has 32 degrees of freedom in its flexible limbs and can both walk and roll. It can drive a car, open doors, and operate power tools. The goal is to make a robot that can deal with complex disaster sites, such as a collapsed building or damaged nuclear reactor.

AUTONOMY
MEDIUM

DRC-Hubo is designed to navigate complex disaster sites with some help from a human controller.

WALK OR ROLL
DRC-Hubo can convert from walking to rolling for greater stability.

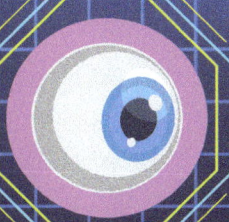

SEEING KNEES
DRC-Hubo has cameras in its shins, to better see where it's going.

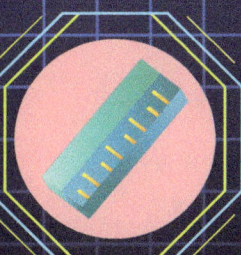

SIZE
DRC-Hubo weighs 176 pounds (80 kilograms) and stands 5.5 feet (1.7 meters) tall.

OLYMPIC RELAY
In 2018, DRC-Hubo became the first robot to ever carry the Olympic torch, in the relay before the Winter Games in PyeongChang, South Korea.

MAKER
Researchers at the Korea Advanced Institute of Science and Technology (KAIST).

Air and Liquid Power

Electric motors are not the only kinds of **actuators** used to make robots move. Some robots have **hydraulic actuators.** In a hydraulic actuator, the power is provided by a pressurized liquid, rather than an electric current.

Jurassic hydraulics
For the movie *Jurassic Park III*, the movie makers built a huge animatronic Spinosaurus robot. It moves entirely with hydraulics, to give a more fluid, natural feel.

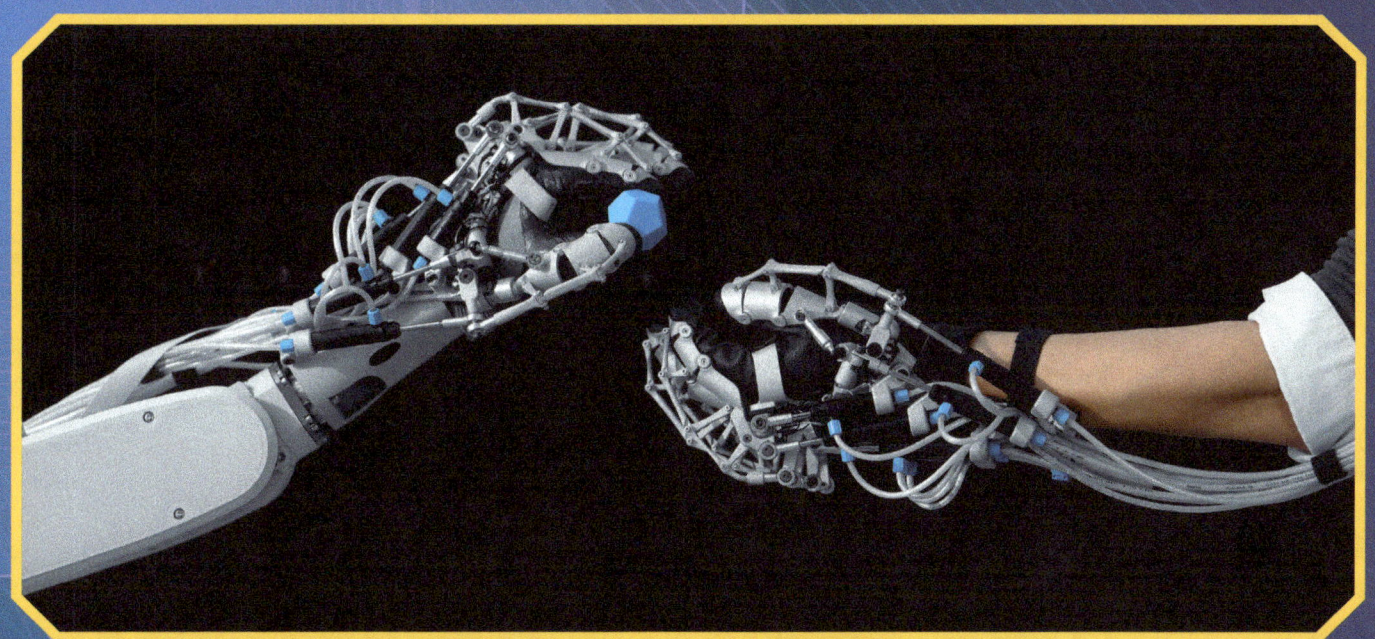

The ExoHand robotic hand uses pneumatic (air-powered) actuators to copy the fluid motions of the human hand.

A simple hydraulic actuator consists of a piston, or rod, housed in a cylinder partially filled with pressurized fluid. Pushing more fluid into the cylinder causes the piston to extend, or stick out farther. Removing fluid causes the piston to retract, or go back into the cylinder. These motions can be used to power the movement of a robot. Hydraulic actuators can generate great power, so they may be used in robots designed for heavy work.

Pneumatic actuators are similar, but they are powered by pressurized air, rather than a liquid. Pneumatic actuators can make small, precise movements, often quickly and quietly. For this reason, they are sometimes used to create facial expressions and other precise gestures in lifelike humanoid robots.

Piezoelectrics

Robots use one kind of technology to both sense *and* do. Piezoelectric materials have a unique property—they produce a tiny electric current when they are squeezed or stretched. This makes them useful in touch **sensors.** When something squeezes the sensor, the robot reads the electrical change as a touch. A stronger force generates more electricity, so piezoelectric sensors can measure the force of a grip.

Some piezoelectric materials also work in reverse. They bend or expand when exposed to an electric current. That means they can be used as **actuators. Piezoelectric actuators** produce only small movements, so they're mostly used in small robots, or where motions need to be precise. But unlike an **electric motor,** there are no moving parts to break. Piezoelectric actuators have been used in tiny flying bots and **swarm robots** meant to work together in groups.

> **RoboBee** is an insect-sized 'bot that uses piezoelectric actuators to move its four delicate wings.

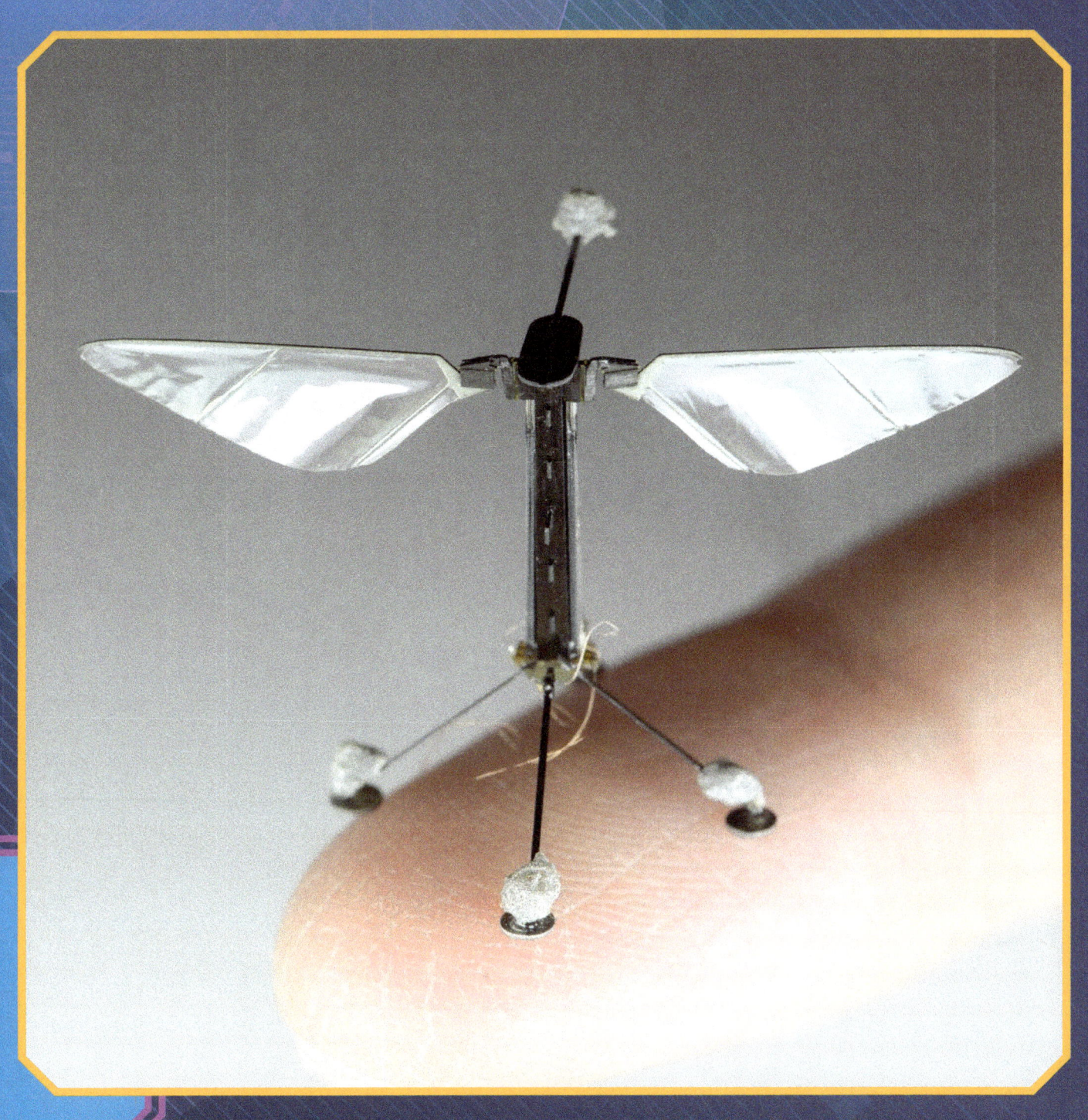

End Effectors

Effectors move—but what do they move? Robots interact with their world through parts called **end effectors.** Imagine your arm was a robotic arm. The end effector would be your hand. You use your hand to grab, hold, and move things.

A robot's hand is sometimes called a **gripper.** But a gripper is only one kind of end effector. A robot's arm might end in a hook, a crushing claw, a welding tool, or any other device you could imagine.

"Can I offer you a drink?" A robot uses devices called end effectors to interact with the outside world. This robot has a gripper modeled after a human hand.

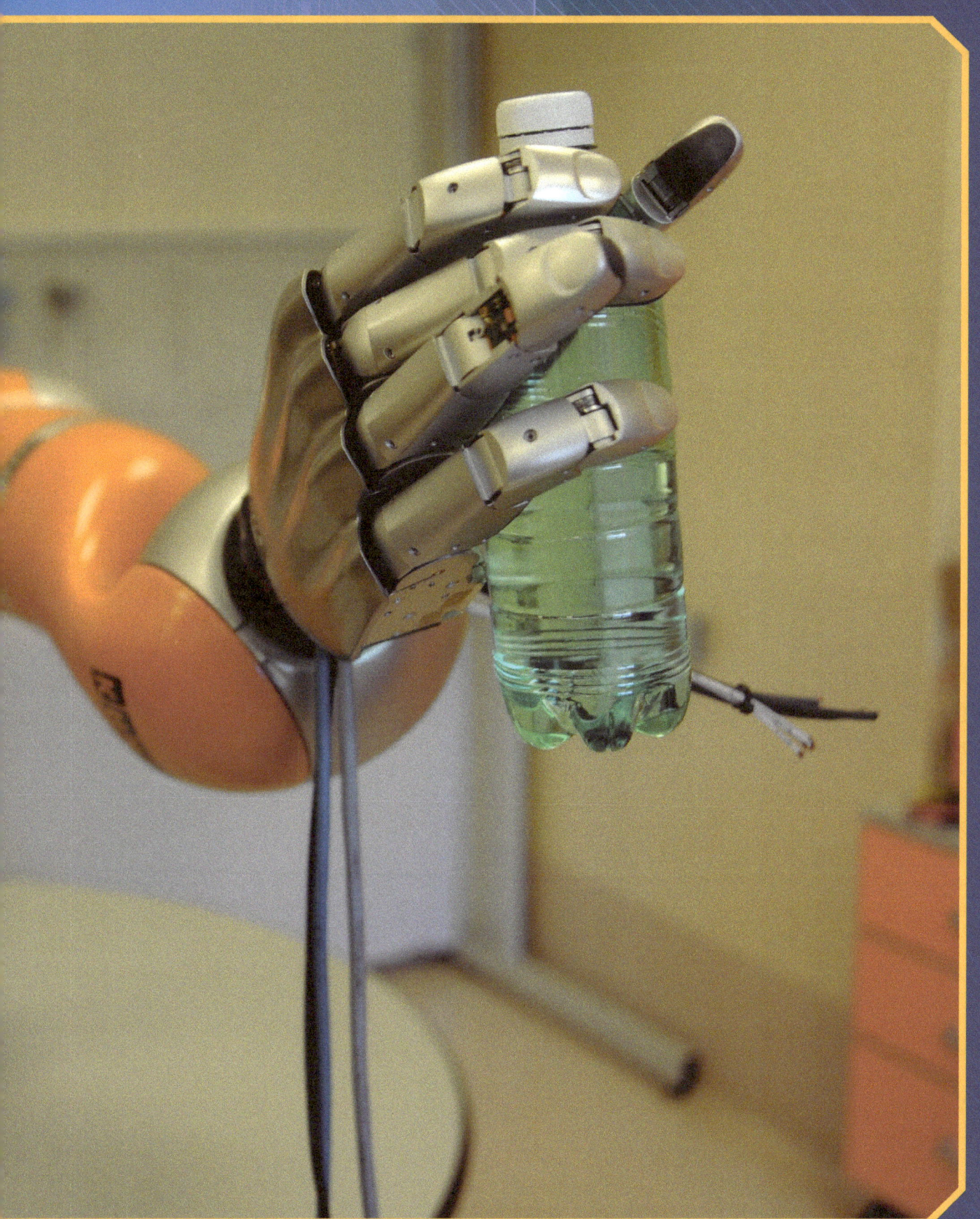

Picking something up—what could be easier? The human hand is an amazing **end effector**, shaped by millions of years of evolution. Robots have been around for less than a hundred years. They can still struggle with a task as simple as picking something up.

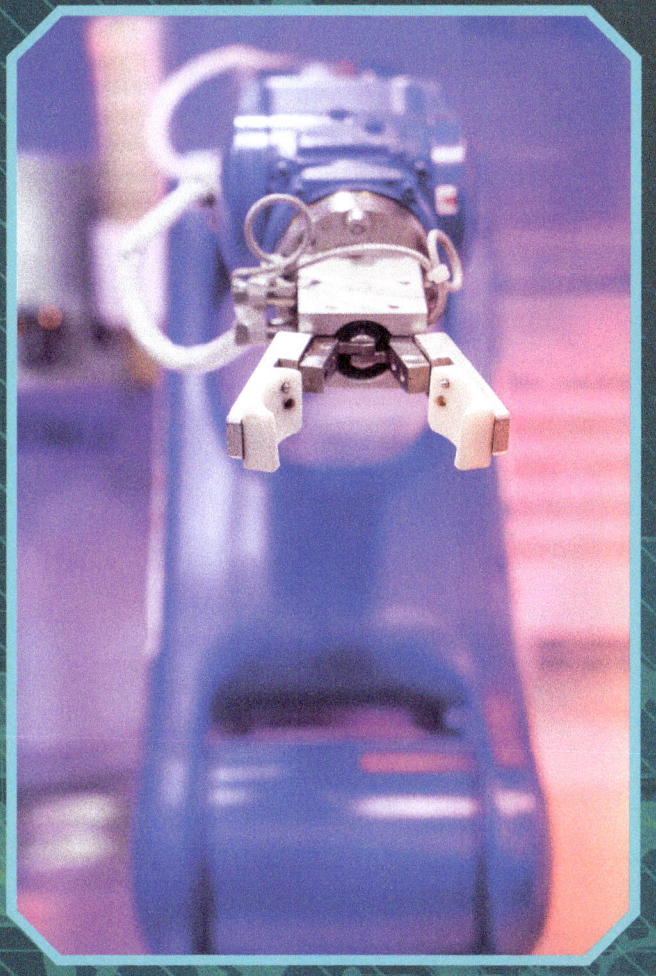

Robots are good at doing the same thing over and over. So it is not surprising that robots were first used in factories. On an assembly line, a robot might handle only one kind of part. But what happens when a robot has to handle objects of different shapes? Imagine a robot designed to sort and box apples. Each apple has its own size and shape—no two are exactly alike.

Worse yet, apples are delicate. A robot that couldn't control its grip strength might end up packing box after box of applesauce.

Grippers

Engineers respond to such challenges by designing different kinds of **grippers.** A simple factory robot might use a basic gripper with two or three fingers. Other industrial robots use the power of suction to pick things up. This allows them to handle more fragile items without crushing them.

A more delicate task—such as packing apples—might call for a soft gripper. Such a gripper uses gentle pressure and flexible fingers to pick up easily damaged objects.

Life is like a box of chocolates, but you always know what you're going to get from this suction gripper: careful, quick packing.

Not all grippers look like hands. In 2010, researchers at Cornell University, the University of Chicago, and iRobot demonstrated a unique "universal gripper." The gripper consists of a balloon filled with coffee grounds. When the gripper is placed against an object, the flexible balloon and shifting grounds mold to the object's shape. Then a vacuum pumps all the air out of the balloon—locking the grains together in a gentle, custom grip.

Magnets can be useful in grippers made to work with metallic parts. Magnetic grippers can even be designed to hold on if the robot loses power.

HELLO, MY NAME IS:

The Shadow Dexterous Hand

Robots come with all kinds of **grippers.** But sometimes, you just need a hand—a human hand. The Shadow Dexterous Hand is the next best thing. The Dexterous Hand is a robot gripper designed to look and act like a human hand. It has four fingers and a thumb, and even comes in right-hand and left-hand models. Ultrasensitive touch sensors on the fingertips allow for a delicate, precision touch.

AUTONOMY
LOW
(It's just a hand!)

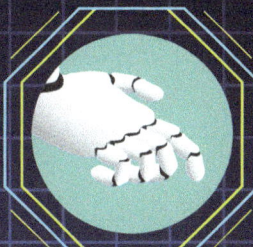

PRECISE TOUCH
The hand is bristling with position and force sensors.

DEXTEROUS INDEED
The Shadow hand has 24 **degrees of freedom,** more than some whole robots.

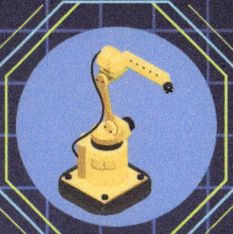

MAKER
The Shadow Robot Company of London, England

WHAT'S IN A NAME?
Dexterous means *skillful,* or *nimble-fingered.*

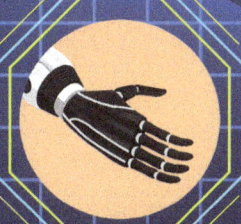

SIZE
The same as a human hand

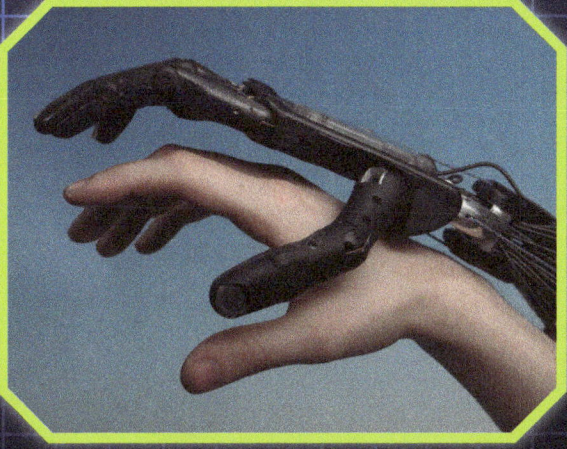

[43]

Other End Effectors

Grippers are just one kind of **end effector.** Other kinds are as unlimited as the jobs that robots do. And robots can be fitted with different end effectors if their tasks change.

A robot working in a factory may have a drill, grinder, or saw as an end effector. Robots with paint guns for end effectors are used to paint automobiles and other manufactured products. Some robots use welders to join two metal parts. Robots with glue gun end effectors are used to assemble many consumer goods.

Firefighting robots might have water or foam cannons, cooks their own spatulas.

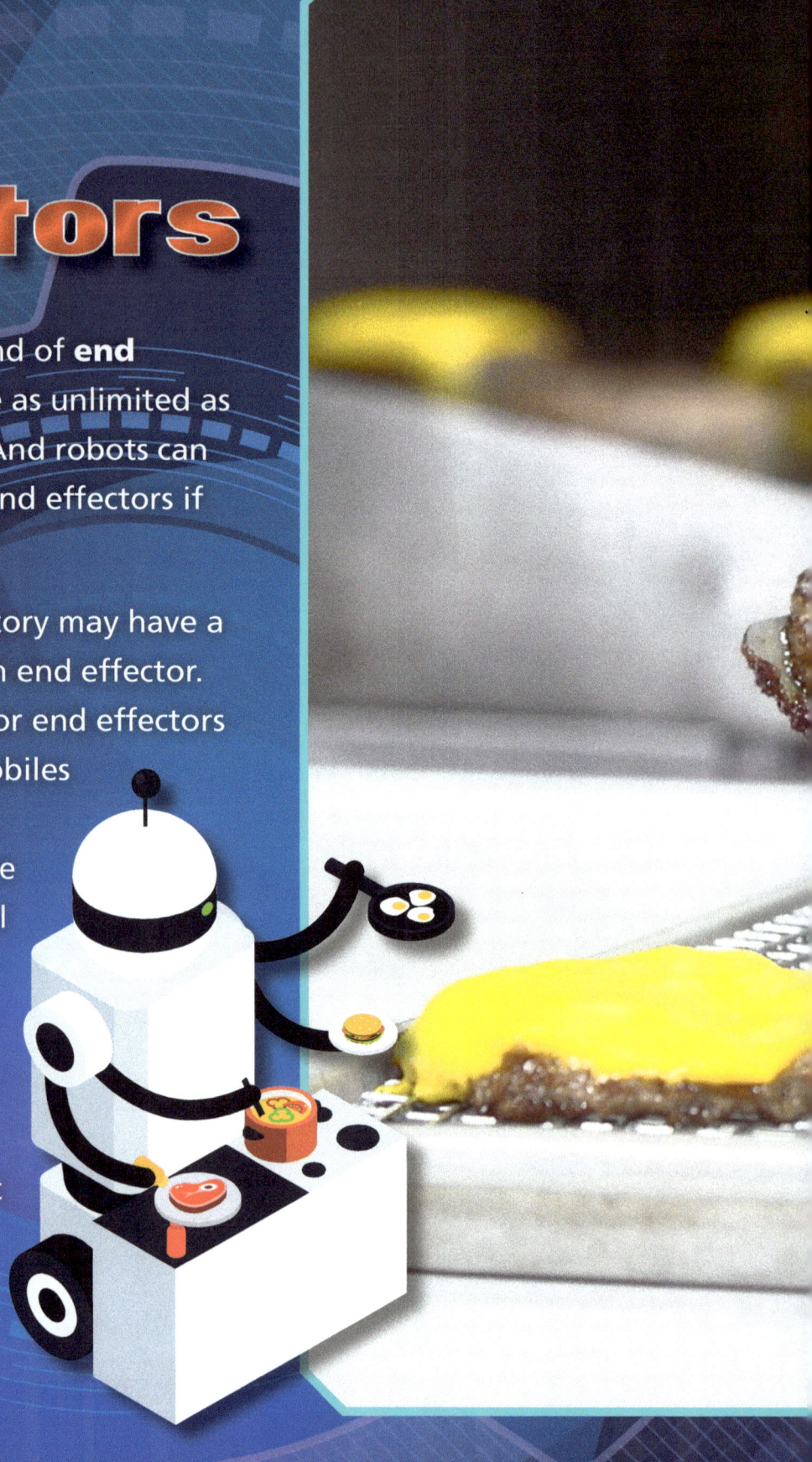

Order up!
A robot called Flippy flips burgers using a spatula as an end effector. Between orders, Flippy switches to a scraper to clean the grill.

Hands-On Robotics

Want to get started making robots? Jump right in!

World Robot Olympiad

The World Robot Olympiad (WRO) is an international robot-building competition that is open to students age 8 to 19. Local contests are held in 95 countries around the world. Students compete within their own age group in different challenges.

In **RoboMission,** teams of 2-3 build and program an autonomous LEGO robot to solve specific challenges on a set field.

In **RoboSports,** teams are free to use any materials to build 'bots to play a sport selected for that year's contest.

For older students, **Future Innovators** challenges teams of 2-3 to construct a robotics solution to a yearly challenge.

Going for gold
Team Romania ready their robot for competition at the 2018 World Robot Olympiad in Chiang Mai, Thailand.

Future Engineers is a contest for high school students to build a robot that responds to a current challenge in robot technology, such as autonomous driving.

The final global competition round is hosted in a different country each year. May the best robots win!

Also check out:
- FIRST Robotics
- RoboCup
- International Robot Olympiad (IROC)
- International Youth Robot Competition

Or ask at your local school, library, or maker space.

Glossary

accelerometer a type of sensor that detects acceleration, whether speeding up, slowing down, or changing direction.

actuator a device, such as a motor, that provides movement to a robot.

artificial intelligence (AI) the ability of a computer system to process information in a manner similar to human thought or to exhibit humanlike behavior.

autonomy the degree to which a robot can make decisions without input from a human operator to achieve a goal.

cliff sensor a type of proximity sensor that detects a sudden drop-off, preventing a robot from falling.

degree of freedom the ability to move in one particular direction at one particular joint. The more degrees of freedom a robot has, the more complex movements it can make.

electric motor a device that produces movement in response to an electric current.

end effector a device a robot uses to interact with its surroundings, generally mounted on the end of a robotic arm.

facial recognition the ability of a machine to identify and remember faces.

gripper a device used for grabbing something; a robot "hand."

gyrometer a sensor that measures rotation.

humanoid shaped like or resembling a human.

hydraulic actuator an actuator powered by a pressurized liquid.

lidar a sensing method in which pulses of laser light are used to measure distances and create three-dimensional pictures of an environment.

piezoelectric actuator an actuator powered by a piece of piezoelectric material, which changes shape in response to an electric current.

pneumatic actuator an actuator powered by compressed air.

proximity sensor a device that detects how near something is.

sensor a device that takes in information from the outside world and translates it into code.

swarm robots small robots designed to work in large groups.

torque turning force.

voice recognition the ability to identify and understand human speech.

Index

A

accelerometers, 24
actuators, 4, 26; hydraulic, 32-33; multiple, 28-29; piezoelectric, 34-35; pneumatic, 33
arms, robotic, 26-29, 36
artificial intelligence (AI), 13
Atlas (robot), 29
autonomy, 19, 31, 43

B

brains, human, 13

C

cameras, 22
cliff sensors, 8, 10-11
cooking robots, 44-45
Cornell University, 41

D

degrees of freedom, 28-30, 43
DRC-Hubo (robot), 30-31

E

electric motors, 4, 26, 28, 32, 34
end effectors, 36-37, 44-45. See also grippers
ExoHand (robot), 33

F

facial recognition, 14-15
Flippy (robot), 45

G

grippers, 36-37; problems with, 38-39; robotic hand, 42-43; types of, 40-41; universal, 41
gyrometers, 24

H

hands, robotic. See grippers
HEARBO (robot), 20-21
Honda Research Institute, 20
humanoid robots, 20-21, 24, 29
hydraulic actuators, 32-33

I

iCub (robot), 4-5
inventory counting, 18-19
iRobot (company), 41

J

Jurassic Park III (movie), 32

K

Korea Advanced Institute of Science and Technology (KAIST) (company), 31

L

lidar, 16-17
light, 6, 10, 16
listening, robotic, 20-21

M

magnets, 41
MetraLabs (company), 19
microphones, 10, 20, 22
muscles, 4, 26

N

Nao (robot), 24-25

P

Pepper (robot), 15
piezoelectric actuators, 34-35
pistons, 33
pneumatic actuators, 33
proprioception, 7
proximity sensors, 10, 13, 16

R

RFID, 18
RoboBee (robot), 35

S

senses, 4, 22
sensors, 4, 6-7; artificial hand, 42, 43; bumper, 8-9; cliff, 8, 10-11; external, 22; internal, 22-25; lidar, 16, 18; microphone, 20; proximity, 10, 13, 16
Shadow Dexterous Hand, 42-43
swarm robots, 34

T

torque, 22, 24
Tory (robot), 18-19

U

ultrasound, 8
University of Chicago, 41

V

vacuum cleaners, robotic, 8-9, 11, 23
vision, robotic, 13-17
voice recognition, 20

W

World Robot Olympiad, 46-47